What are nature's copycats?

Big
Science Ideas

Bobbie Kalman

Crabtree Publishing Company
www.crabtreebooks.com

Big Science Ideas

Created by Bobbie Kalman

for Tessa DeRocco,
an awesome future librarian who loves to read
and help out in the school library

Author and
Editor-in-Chief
Bobbie Kalman

Editor
Kathy Middleton

Proofreader
Crystal Sikkens

Design
Bobbie Kalman
Katherine Berti
Samantha Crabtree
    (logo and front cover)

Photo research
Bobbie Kalman

Print and production coordinator
Katherine Berti

Prepress technician
Katherine Berti

Photographs
Dreamstime: page 18 (bottom)
iStockPhoto: page 18 (top)
Wikimedia Commons: John: page 19 (top);
    Nick Hobgood: page 20 (inset)
All other images by Shutterstock

Library and Archives Canada Cataloguing in Publication

Kalman, Bobbie
    What are nature's copycats? / Bobbie Kalman.

(Big science ideas)
Includes index.
Issued also in electronic formats.
ISBN 978-0-7787-2771-2 (bound).--ISBN 978-0-7787-2776-7 (pbk.)

    1. Camouflage (Biology)--Juvenile literature. 2. Mimicry
(Biology)--Juvenile literature. I. Title. II. Series: Kalman,
Bobbie. Big science ideas

QL767.K34 2012   j591.47'2   C2011-907683-7

Library of Congress Cataloging-in-Publication Data

Kalman, Bobbie.
    What are nature's copycats? / Bobbie Kalman.
        p. cm. -- (Big science ideas)
    Includes index.
    ISBN 978-0-7787-2771-2 (reinforced library binding : alk. paper) --
ISBN 978-0-7787-2776-7 (pbk. : alk. paper) -- ISBN 978-1-4271-7840-4
(electronic pdf) -- ISBN 978-1-4271-7955-5 (electronic html)
    1. Camouflage (Biology)--Juvenile literature. 2. Mimicry (Biology)--
Juvenile literature. I. Title.

QL767.K356 2012
591.47'2--dc23
                                                    2011046110

Crabtree Publishing Company

Printed in Canada/012012/MA20111130

www.crabtreebooks.com   1-800-387-7650

Published in Canada
Crabtree Publishing
616 Welland Ave.
St. Catharines, Ontario
L2M 5V6

Published in the United States
Crabtree Publishing
PMB 59051
350 Fifth Avenue, 59th Floor
New York, New York 10118

Published in the United Kingdom
Crabtree Publishing
Maritime House
Basin Road North, Hove
BN41 1WR

Published in Australia
Crabtree Publishing
3 Charles Street
Coburg North
VIC 3058

Contents

Why do they hide?

Animals need to find food to **survive**, or stay alive. Some animals hunt and eat other animals. These hunters are called **predators**. The animals they hunt are called **prey**. Both predators and prey use **camouflage** to hide. Camouflage is colors or markings that allow an animal to blend in with its surroundings. Camouflage hides predators so they can sneak up on their prey. It also hides prey so that predators cannot easily see and eat them.

The colors and patterns on the body of this fish help it blend in with the plants and animals in the ocean. If you were swimming in the ocean, do you think you could see this fish?

Nature's copycats

Some animals are hidden because they **mimic**, or copy, parts of their surroundings. This kind of camouflage is called **mimicry**. Animals that use mimicry are often very hard to see because they look like other parts of nature, like leaves, sticks, rocks, tree bark, coral, flowers, or other animals. Mimics are nature's copycats. You can find them on land and under water.

Leafy seadragons mimic seaweed floating in water (see page 27).

This orchid mantis looks like a flower (see pages 10–11).

It's good to be green!

Many insects and other animals that live in forests, grasses, or among plants with green leaves are green themselves. For example, some lizards, frogs, snakes, and caterpillars are green. Green is the only color they need to blend in with their surroundings. Some of these animals are predators, and some are prey. Some use the color green as camouflage. Others are also mimics, or copycats, that look like parts of their surroundings.

This green caterpillar is the same color as the leaves it eats. It is well camouflaged by its green color.

This green frog blends in with the green leaves in its **habitat**. Its habitat is the natural place where it lives.

This green tree python lives in a rain forest. It is a predator that hides among the green leaves of trees.

This insect is a katydid. Katydids are known as long-horned grasshoppers, but they are more like crickets. Katydids are excellent mimics. This one looks just like the green leaf underneath it.

Leaves and sticks

Some insects are predators, and some are prey. When they mimic the leaves, flowers, or sticks around them, it is very hard to see them. Some look like green leaves, and some look like autumn leaves that have just fallen from trees. Some even have dark edges that make them look like dead leaves. Other insects resemble thin sticks or parts of thick tree branches.

The dead-looking leaf above and this sticklike insect are both praying mantises. These insects mimic many parts of nature. Learn more about them on pages 10–11.

Stick insects look like parts of tree or bush branches.

These katydids are mimicking a green and a brown leaf.

Leaf insects are the best leaf mimics! They look exactly like leaves. Some are green, and others are yellow, orange, or brown—the colors of autumn leaves. These insects even rock back and forth to look like leaves being blown by the wind. The three insects below are leaf insects.

Masters of mimicry

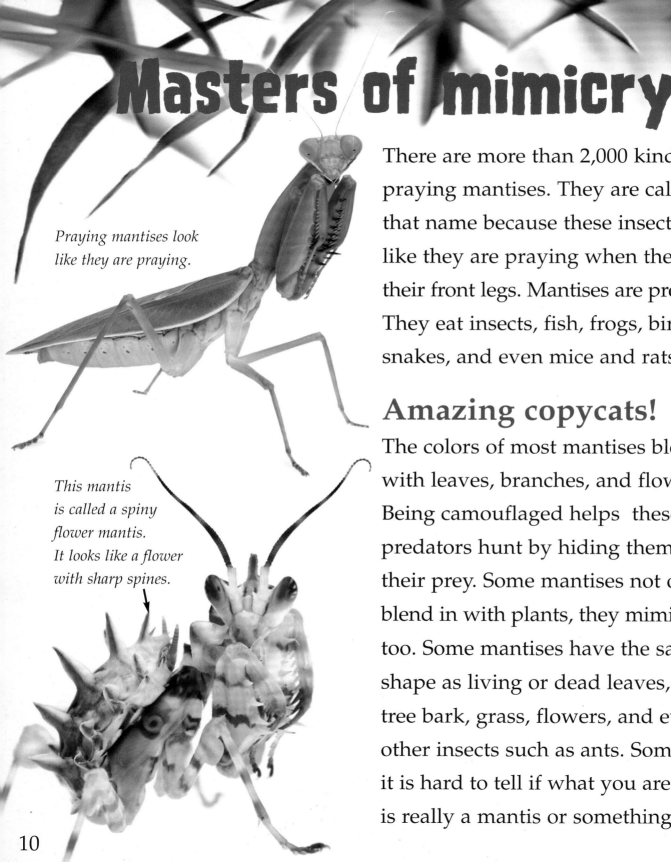

Praying mantises look like they are praying.

This mantis is called a spiny flower mantis. It looks like a flower with sharp spines.

There are more than 2,000 kinds of praying mantises. They are called by that name because these insects look like they are praying when they fold their front legs. Mantises are predators. They eat insects, fish, frogs, birds, snakes, and even mice and rats.

Amazing copycats!

The colors of most mantises blend in with leaves, branches, and flowers. Being camouflaged helps these predators hunt by hiding them from their prey. Some mantises not only blend in with plants, they mimic them, too. Some mantises have the same shape as living or dead leaves, sticks, tree bark, grass, flowers, and even other insects such as ants. Sometimes it is hard to tell if what you are seeing is really a mantis or something else.

eyespot

The wings of some mantises have
stripes and big **eyespots**. This mantis
looks like a ballet dancer, but it is not
dancing. It is standing tall, with its
legs spread, and its wings opened wide.
This pose makes the mantis seem larger
and more scary to predators.

11

Butterfly mimics

There are two kinds of butterflies on this page. One is a monarch butterfly, and the other is a viceroy butterfly. They have the same colors and patterns, but the viceroy has an extra black stripe across the bottom part of its wings. Monarchs are poisonous, and birds that eat a lot of them can die. The viceroy can make predators sick, but it is not as poisonous as the monarch. The viceroy mimics the coloring of the monarch to seem more dangerous to predators. Mimicry saves both kinds of butterflies because predators learn not to eat either one. How many monarchs are there? How many viceroys?

monarch butterfly

viceroy butterfly

What big eyes!

Some butterflies and other insects, such as mantises, have huge eyespots on their bodies. Eyespots do not scare predators because they look like eyes, but the colors and patterns on the wings of the butterflies do confuse them. Predators may think an owl butterfly is an owl when they see the butterfly upside down.

owl butterfly

owl eyes

The beautiful peacock butterfly also has large eyespots to fool predators. The spots may make predators think the butterfly is bigger than it really is.

13

Caterpillar copycats

Many animals eat caterpillars, but a caterpillar's appearance can often keep predators away. Markings and certain body parts can hide a caterpillar, make it seem bigger than it is, or cause it to be dangerous to eat. Many caterpillars look like the plants on which they feed. They may even have parts that mimic plant parts. Some caterpillars have spiny bristles or long fine hairs that come off on the skin of predators. The bristles can cause pain or even kill predators because some contain poison.

The caterpillar on the left has long hairs that some predators cannot swallow. The caterpillar below is mimicking the branch on which it is crawling. It also has sharp horns.

Some caterpillars
have long whips at
the ends of their bodies.
The caterpillars wiggle
these to scare away
other insects or animals.

The saddleback caterpillar
has poisonous spines that
can harm predators.

The caterpillar above is
eating parts of a flower.
It has spikes that look
sharp and dangerous.

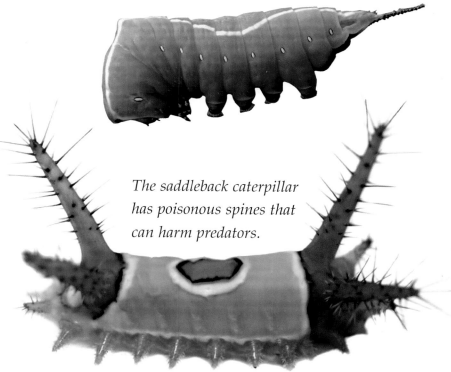

The **osmeterium**, or double horn, of swallowtail caterpillars can give off a terrible smell!
The stripes of the monarch caterpillar warn predators that this caterpillar tastes
very bad. Predators do not want to eat animals that smell or taste bad.

monarch caterpillar

osmeterium

swallowtail
caterpillar

Frog mimics

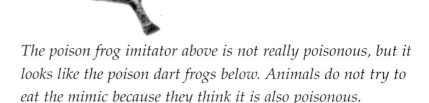

Bright **warning colors** and markings let predators know that an animal is dangerous. Poison dart frogs, for example, are the most poisonous animals on Earth. Their bright colors and patterns tell other animals that these frogs have poison in their bodies. Most animals, except a few kinds of snakes, die if they eat these frogs. Some tree frogs are not poisonous, but they look like they are. They have similar patterns and colors as those of poison dart frogs.

The poison frog imitator above is not really poisonous, but it looks like the poison dart frogs below. Animals do not try to eat the mimic because they think it is also poisonous.

lichen

Can you see the frog in the picture above? This frog is called a moss frog or bush frog. It lives in China. Its body is covered in bumps that look like the **lichens** and **mosses** that grow on tree bark.

lichen

moss

Many frogs and toads have bright colors or patterns on their bellies or thighs. The fire-bellied toad has a bright red underside. When it sees a predator, it flashes its bright color to startle the animal and make it back off. The toad then has time to escape.

Reptile copycats

Reptiles are animals that are covered in **scales**. Scales are bony plates. Reptiles include lizards, alligators and crocodiles, and snakes. The animal shown above and below is a leaf-tailed gecko. Leaf-tailed geckos are small lizards found only in Madagascar, an island country that is part of Africa. These geckos live on trees and mimic tree bark exactly, as well as the mosses and lichens growing on it. Their tails are shaped like leaves.

This leaf-tailed gecko looks just like the tree trunk on which it lives. Its tail mimics a dying leaf.

coral snake

Poison!

Like frogs and many lizards, snakes are predators, and many are poisonous. Some poisonous snakes, such as the coral snake, have large bands of red, white or yellow, and black on their bodies. These colors are warning signs to other predators, such as eagles and hawks, to stay away.

milk snake

Milk snakes mimic coral snakes, but they are not poisonous. Predators cannot tell which snake is which, but you can, if you remember, "Red next to yellow, dangerous fellow. Red next to black, will not hurt Jack."

Coral reef cleaners

Warm oceans have colorful habitats called **coral reefs**. Coral reefs are made up of animals called **coral polyps**. Many kinds of fish and other animals hide in the colorful corals. Both predators and prey use mimicry to find food and stay safe.

This small fish, called the blue-lined saber-toothed blenny, may look harmless, but it is a mimic that can do serious damage to much bigger fish! Read the next page to find out how.

Cleaner fish

Coral reef animals go to **cleaning stations** to be cleaned by small **cleaner fish**. Cleaner fish eat dead skin, as well as **parasites** that live on bigger fish. Getting cleaned helps keep these animals healthy and feeds the cleaners at the same time.

Striped mimics

Cleaner fish have stripes along the length of their bodies and do a "dance" to let fish know that they are cleaners. Some are not cleaners, however. They are cleaner mimics! The blue-lined saber-toothed blenny is a mimic that pretends to be a cleaner. Instead of eating dead skin, it takes bites out of the flesh of the fish it pretends to clean.

Cleaner wrasses are cleaning this giant moray eel. The eel is allowing them to swim inside its mouth. Are the wrasses real cleaners or mimics?

Octopus copycats

Octopuses can change the colors and patterns on their bodies to blend in with different parts of their habitats. They can even make their skin look bumpy or smooth to match their surroundings. The octopus below is the same as the one at the top of the opposite page, but its colors are different in the different surroundings. Octopuses have **pigments** in their skin that allow them to change colors. A pigment is a natural color found in plants and animals.

The octopus is now well hidden by the corals around it. It is much lighter in color than it is on page 22.

lionfish

mimic octopus

The mimic octopus on the right can copy the looks and movements of fifteen sea animals, including sea snakes, giant crabs, stingrays, sea jellies, and lionfish (shown above). It does this by changing color and twisting its body and arms into different poses.

Can you see them?

Some undersea animals are almost invisible. They seem to be made of glass. Predators and prey may not see these **transparent**, or see-through, animals. The colors around them show through their bodies and make the animals seem to disappear. Sea jellies, glass fish, anemone shrimp, and deep-sea octopuses mimic being invisible.

This anemone shrimp is well camouflaged among the tentacles of a sea anemone. The shrimp is prey to many animals when it can be seen. Can you see it in the picture? Describe how you think it looks.

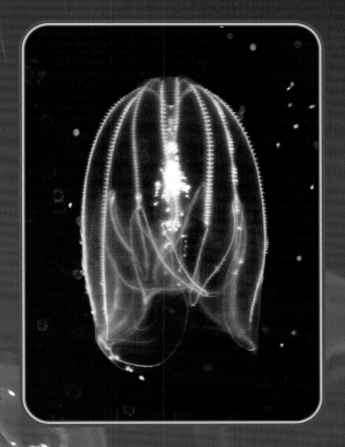

Glass fish are almost transparent— even when they swim in groups.

Sea jellies

There are sea jellies behind the pictures on both these pages. They are almost invisible in the ocean because their bodies are transparent. The sea jelly in the photo above lives in the deepest part of the ocean. It makes its own light. The light attracts prey. When prey swims to the light, the sea jelly catches and eats it.

Deep-sea octopuses can look transparent in dark ocean waters.

How do they mimic?

The heads of sea horses look like tiny horse heads from the side. These fish are poor swimmers, so they usually stay in one place with their tails wound around a piece of coral. Sea horses can mimic the coral to which they are attached. They can have colorful patterns and growths or even look like totally different creatures.

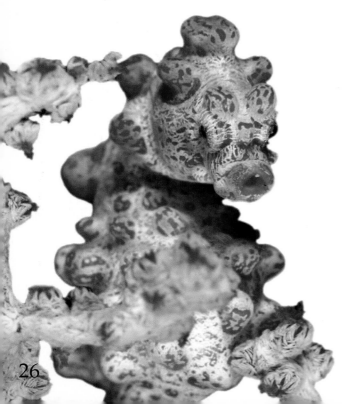

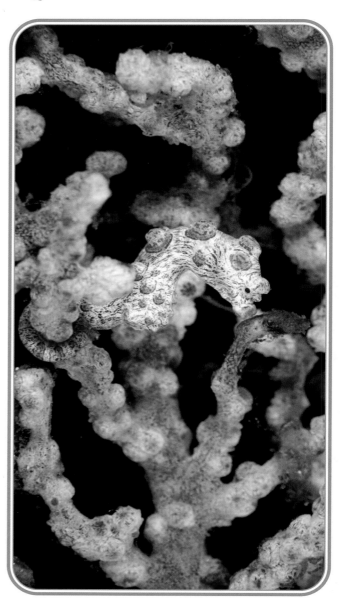

The pygmy sea horse above matches the pink bumpy coral around it. These sea horses are so good at hiding that people discovered them only about ten years ago! Where is the one in the picture above?

Leafy seadragons belong to the seahorse family, but they are slightly bigger than most sea horses. The leafy skin growths of these fish look just like seaweed. Leafy seadragons even move through water like pieces of floating seaweed.

Ghost pipefish are also related to sea horses. They float upside down and find their food on the bottom of reefs. They are almost impossible to see because they blend in so well with colorful corals. Find their heads and eyes.

Talking birds

Some birds can mimic sounds in nature. They can copy the songs of other birds or even some sounds made by people. There are some birds that can "talk" like humans and understand the meanings of words. Most crows, mynas, parrots, budgies, and starlings are able to imitate human words. Some can learn to imitate words in different languages. In fact, parrots can even say words in up to twenty languages!

Blue-and-yellow macaws are big parrots that often "scream" and make other loud noises. They can learn to say many words and even sing songs.

African gray parrots can imitate the calls of several other kinds of birds. They are also able to say hundreds of human words and understand what the words mean. They can even copy the voices of different people.

28

Starlings can imitate the sounds made by 15–20 birds. They also imitate a few sounds other than those of wild birds, such as human voices and sounds made by cars and other machines.

The myna belongs to the starling family. Some mynas are talking birds. As pets, they have learned to mimic human speech.

Male budgerigars, or budgies, are believed to be one of the top five talking parrot champions. A budgie named Puck learned to say 1,728 words!

Listen!

You can hear birds talk on YouTube. Just search for the bird you want to hear, and listen!

Which are the mimics?

Some animals have colors, patterns, or textures that remind people of other animals. The pairs of animals shown on these pages may be similar in some ways, but are they mimics? Mimics live in the same habitats and copy plants or animals that help them survive. Which of these animals are true mimics, and which are not?

hornet

*Hornets visit flowers to find insects to eat. Hoverflies eat the **nectar** and **pollen** found in flowers. Hoverflies look just like hornets, but they do not sting.*

hoverfly

The gecko below is a leopard gecko. It is named after the leopard because of its spots. Are the two animals mimics of each other?

leopard

leopard gecko

zebra longwing
butterfly

porcupine
fish

Is the zebra
longwing
butterfly a
copycat of
the zebra?

zebra

Porcupines have sharp quills, and so do
porcupine fish. One lives in a forest, and
the other in the ocean. Are they mimics?

porcupine

Answer

The only mimic is the hoverfly, which
is also called a hornet mimic. Predators
stay away from it because it looks like
a hornet, whose stings are very painful.

31

Glossary

Note: Some boldfaced words are defined where they appear in the book.

camouflage Colors or markings on an animal that hide it in its natural surroundings

cleaning station A location in a reef where sea animals are cleaned by small fish such as wrasses

coral reef An area in shallow ocean water that is made up of live and dead corals

eyespot A marking on an animal, which looks like an eye and confuses predators

lichen A slow-growing crustlike plant that grows on rocks or tree trunks

mimic To look like something else

mimicry A color pattern or growth that makes an animal look like something else in nature

moss A small green plant that grows in moist habitats and has no true roots

nectar A sweet liquid found in flowers

osmeterium Forked horns on some caterpillars that give off a terrible smell

parasite A tiny animal that lives on the bodies of other animals

pigment The material in plant and animal cells that provides color

pollen A powder in flowers that is needed to make new flowers

reptile A cold-blooded animal that lays eggs

scale A small, flat, tough structure on the skin of some animals, such as fish and reptiles

transparent Describing an object that is clear and allows light to shine through it

warning colors Bright colors or patterns on the coats or wings of some animals that warn others that the brightly colored animal is poisonous

Index